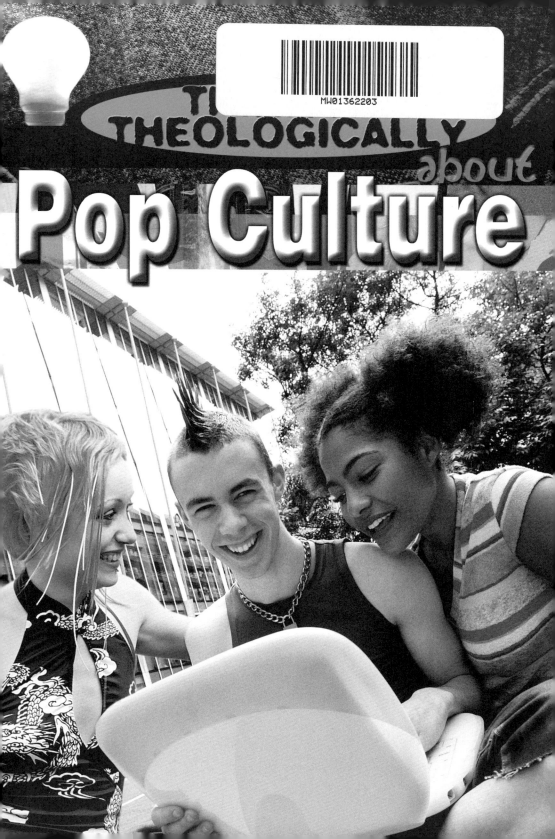

Think THEOLOGICALLY about Pop Culture

THINKING THEOLOGICALLY *about*

POP CULTURE

Copyright © 2004 by Abingdon Press. All rights reserved.

With the exception of those items so noted, no part of this work may be reproduced or transmitted in any form or by any means, electronic or mechanical, including photocopying and recording, or by any information storage or retrieval system, except as may be expressly permitted by the 1976 Copyright Act or in writing from the publisher. Requests for permission should be addressed to Abingdon Press, 201 Eighth Avenue, South, P.O. Box 801, Nashville, TN 37202-0801.

Unless otherwise noted, Scripture quotations are from the *New Revised Standard Version of the Bible,* copyright © 1989, Division of Christian Education of the National Council of the Churches of Christ in the United States of America. Used by permission. All rights reserved.

Cover Design: Keely Moore

MANUFACTURED IN THE UNITED STATES OF AMERICA

08 09 10 11 12 13—10 9 8 7

Contents

Session 1: The Big Picture 7

Session 2: Reason 17

Session 3: Experience 23

Session 4: Scripture 27

Session 5: Tradition 35

Session 6: Thinking Theologically About Pop Culture 43

Writer Bio

A former youth director, Sarah F. Arthur now serves youth as a writer, editor, speaker, and workshop leader. In addition to writing *Thinking Theologically About Money* and *Thinking Theologically About Pop Culture*, Sarah has written curriculum for *LinC* and *Claim the Name*. Her first book, *Walking With Frodo: A Devotional Journey Through the Lord of the Rings* (November 2003), is part of Tyndale House Publisher's new thirsty(?) line for young adults. She also writes fiction and poetry and illustrates her own stories for children. Check out her work on www.saraharthur.com. Sarah and her husband, Tom, live in Petoskey, Michigan.

Sticky-Note Rituals

Rituals are like sticky-notes—they remind us of what's really important. We put them in prominent places so that we won't forget what we need to do each day, each hour, each minute.

That's why we begin and end session with these ritualized sayings from Scripture—to remind us of God's faithfulness and love. God's people have been saying these reminders to one another for centuries.

Opening

Leader: "Lord, you have been our dwelling place in all generations."

Class: "Before the mountains were brought forth, or ever you had formed the earth and the world,"

All: "From everlasting to everlasting you are God."

—From **Psalm 90:1-2**

Closing

Together: "May the God of peace sanctify you entirely; and may your spirit and soul and body be kept sound and blameless at the coming of our Lord Jesus Christ." Amen.

—From **1 Thessalonians 5:23**

SESSION 1 — The Big Picture

What's Hot, What's Not

For the next few weeks we will be studying "pop culture"—a short-hand way of saying "popular culture." So what is popular culture, anyway?

- **Popular:** that which is most dominant, accepted, valued, or accessible by the general population

- **Culture:** the unique ways that a group of people defines itself. Aspects of culture include language, dress, customs, beliefs, values, leisure, entertainment, and artistic expression (music, art, literature, and so forth).

Based on the above definitions, what do you think "pop culture" is? Give some examples.

Extra credit: How many unique cultures can you identify in your school or community? Which one would you say is the most dominant or the most popular?

Anthropology 101

- **Anthropology:** the study of human cultures

Anthropologists use the word *culture* to refer to different tribes and people groups, both past and present, around the world. Anthropologists study the various aspects of a group's culture to determine how it differs from others and its unique contributions to the advancement or preservation of human life. They study East African culture, ancient Bronze Age culture, Colonial American culture, and post-World-War II Japanese culture. And yes, they even study present-day American "pop culture"!

> "God made humans and purposed them to carry on [God's] creative work by *doing culture*,

As Christians, it is important for us to be able to step back and look at our culture from God's perspective. We must look at the big picture.

Made in God's Image
Because we are made in God's image as creators who can express our uniqueness, we know that some aspects of culture are good: some aspects of culture reflect God's image and give us glimpses of God's grace.

Where do you see glimpses of God or biblical values in today's pop culture? Think about the posters on your wall—either at home, in the church building, or elsewhere.

Sinful People
Because humans are sinful, many aspects of human cultures are sinful. These aspects demonstrate a rejection of God and God's ways and a commitment to selfish pursuits.

Where do you see proof of sin and selfish values in pop culture? Again, think about the posters on your wall at home, in the church building, or elsewhere.

Striking a Balance
As Christians, we have to strike a balance. We must learn to challenge rather than accept those aspects of pop culture that are ungodly while embracing those that reflect an honest search for God. We are also called to actively influence pop culture so that it will better reflect our Christian values.

fashioning ways of life that promote love, kindness, mercy, justice, truth, and stewardship."
—William Romanowski

Theo-WHAT?

Living the Christian life involves two very important questions:

- How do we know what God thinks about an issue?
- How do we know what God wants us to do about that issue?

That is the essence of theology, or "the study of God."

- ***Theo***: the Greek word for God
- ***ology***: the Greek suffix for "the study of"

In this study we will be asking these two questions about the issue of pop culture. In other words we'll be "thinking theologically" about pop culture.

theology— the study of God

discern— to distinguish; to have clearness of mental sight

theological framework— a system or method for understanding God's truth. It gives shape and structure to an issue the way a frame gives shape to a house.

Thinking Theologically

Several centuries ago, an Anglican minister named John Wesley gave his people a practical way of deciding—or discerning—God's view on any given topic, including the culture of the day.

A careful study of Wesley's writings and sermons gives us a four-step theological framework for discerning God's perspective.

This framework helps us discover how God wants us to act. As a four-wall framework gives shape and stability to a house, Wesley's four-step framework gives us a reliable method for discerning the truth. The steps are Scripture, experience, reason, and tradition. This method is called the Wesleyan Quadrilateral.

The Wesleyan Quadrilateral

 **Scripture**

The Bible is God's Word for our lives, and it contains everything we need for salvation in Jesus Christ. Scripture is our primary guide for faith and practice. In it we witness God's loving intent throughout the history of God's people; through the life, death, and resurrection of Jesus; and through the Spirit-empowered history of the early church. And by it we are shown how to be purposeful members of the kingdom of God in the here and now.

 **Experience**

Experience—the trials and joys of real life—tests and molds our Christian beliefs. It brings to life the truths revealed in Scripture. Experience is the one step that is truly your own. It gives each person's faith a unique flavor.

 **Reason**

Reason is the ability we all have to ask questions and arrive at conclusions using our intellect. Our minds are gifts from God. The Christian faith is a worldview held by intelligent, thinking people of all walks of life.

 **Tradition**

Tradition is our faith heritage: the common practices and beliefs of the Christian church throughout the centuries.

"We hear God's story through Bible and tradition. We tell our stories through reason and experience."

—Robert K. Johnston

Things to Keep in Mind

Wesley believed that Scripture is the most important step in the theological process, though the other three steps are still necessary.

Why should we use all four components of the Quadrilateral when discerning the truth—not just "reason" or "experience" alone?

- If we use our reason alone, we might come to rely on all sorts of lofty theories that have never been tested.

- If we use our experience alone, we might rely too much on our own finite perspective, which is tainted by sin.

- If we use the traditions of the church alone, we might limit the work of the Holy Spirit or ignore the fact that the history of the church is also tainted with sin.

- And if we take little bits of Scripture alone, we may never know the broader biblical story or understand each passage in its historical and cultural contexts.

We must put all four components of the Quadrilateral together to get a comprehensive Christian understanding of any topic, including pop culture.

Movie Review

Watch the movie clip. As you watch, keep in mind your assigned step from the Wesleyan Quadrilateral (one of the four below). Then use your step to respond to the message of the movie.

Experience

- What have you or others experienced that relates to the events portrayed in this scene? In other words, does this clip accurately represent life as you know it? Why or why not?

- Will this scene stick in your mind for weeks to come? Why or why not? Is that a good or a bad thing?

- When has a movie influenced you to act or be a certain way? Does this movie have that kind of effect? If so, is its influence positive or negative?

- Based on experience, how much should you let the message of this movie influence your thoughts, actions, or words?

Reason

- If you were to walk into a public place and do or say the things that the characters in this movie did or said, what would happen?

- Based on this scene, what message do you think this movie is trying to get across? What are your thoughts on that message?

- How necessary was the behavior or speech of the characters in getting across the point of the movie? In other words, did you have to see and hear every little detail in order to get the point, or could the story have been told differently?

- Should you judge the whole movie based on this scene? Why or why not?

Scripture

- What values are at play in this scene? In other words, what do the characters think is important? What are the characters trying to achieve?

- How are these values consistent or inconsistent with what Jesus says in Matthew 22:36-40?

- What specific biblical commandments are broken in this scene (look up Deuteronomy 5:6-21)?

- Based on Scripture, how well (or badly) does this scene reflect a Christian approach to life?

Tradition

- Would the people in your congregation or denomination affirm or condemn the behaviors depicted in this scene? Why?

- Would their opinion of the behaviors depicted in this scene keep the people in your congregation or denomination from watching this particular movie? Why or why not?

- Would people in your congregation or denomination recommend this movie to others? Why or why not?

- What roles do popular movies or music play in your church's worship service, if any? If none, why?

Case Study, A.D. 5050

It is the year A.D. 5050. You and a highly specialized team of anthropologists have been asked by the Global Federation of Nations to research the culture of ancient twenty-first century America to determine why the word *Britney* appears so often in artifacts from the early part of the third millennium. Was Britney a military leader? a political figure? a religious icon? You have only limited access to an archive of ancient artifacts that includes three personal computer hard drives, several CDs and DVDs, fragments of magazine manuscripts, and a handful of disintegrating articles of clothing. Based on these items, you are able to prepare the following report. Answer the questions on a separate sheet of paper:

Report #1

- **Speech:** What special words or phrases did twenty-first century American people use?

- **Dress:** What did they wear (males as well as females)?

- **Customs:** How did they behave?

- **Music:** What was their music like? What were its messages?

- **Literature:** What were they reading? What were its messages?

- **Art:** What images, decorations, or accessories did they have around? What does this tell you about their tastes?

- **Entertainment:** What did they do for fun during their leisure time?

- **Values:** What did they think was important? What were their goals in life?

- **Beliefs:** What did they believe about family? faith? education? work? money? relationships? suffering?

Based on your report, what is your best guess as to why the word *Britney* appears so often in artifacts from the early part of the third millennium?

What do your findings say about the people who lived at that time?

Report #2

The Archbishop of the Global Parish A.D. 5050 has asked your team to further assess the values and beliefs of twenty-first century Americans. The Archbishop wants to know:

- What was the role of the Christian faith in the popular culture of that time?

- How often did the average person go to church? read the Bible? pray?

- How were Christians portrayed in the popular entertainment media of the day (on television, in movies, on the Internet, and so forth)?

- How did the culture of that time reflect godly, biblical values?

- How did it reflect sinful, selfish values?

Make your best guess in answering the above questions. Then summarize: Based on this report, how much did Christian values and beliefs influence the popular culture of ancient twenty-first century America?

Think About It!

- How does something or someone become popular?

- Who determines what's popular and what's not?

- Do you generally agree or disagree with popular opinion? Why?

- How does it feel to know that what is popular today may not be popular tomorrow? Does this knowledge affect how you interact with popular persons or trends? (For example, does it affect how you spend your money or how you invest your time and energy?)

- What does God have to say about what's "hot" and what's not?

- Whose opinion matters most to you: yours, others', or God's? Why?

Read Colossians 3:1-3.

Reflect: Pop culture has been part of every generation, but it's always changing. What's popular today may not be popular tomorrow. But as Christians, we are called to focus on those things that have eternal value, not just temporary value. We are to live as persons who belong to the eternal kingdom of God.

SESSION 2: Mix and Match

Reason

Did you know that only a handful of media conglomerates own almost all or part of the major TV networks, film production companies, magazines, record companies, publishing houses, movie theaters, and radio stations in the USA?[1] It may seem like you get to choose what you want when it comes to news and entertainment, but the truth is that a handful of executives are making those choices for you.

The major conglomerates are:
- Viacom
- Disney
- News Corp
- Time Warner
- Sony

Their companies are (and this is just the tip of the iceberg!):

Broadcasting
- ABC (Disney)
- Cartoon Network (Time Warner)
- CBS (Viacom)
- CNN (Time Warner)
- Comedy Central (Viacom and Time Warner)
- The Disney Channel (Disney)
- ESPN (Disney with Hearst)
- FOX (News Corp)
- fx (News Corp)
- HBO (Time Warner)
- The Movie Channel (Viacom)
- MTV (Viacom)
- Nickelodeon (Viacom)
- Spike TV (Viacom)
- TBS (Time Warner)
- TNT (Time Warner)
- TV Guide Channel (News Corp)
- VH1 (Viacom)
- WB Television (Time Warner)

Magazines
- *MAD Magazine* (Time Warner)
- *TV Guide* (News Corp)
- *Time* (Time Warner)
- *People* (Time Warner)
- *Discover* (Disney)
- *Sports Illustrated* (Time Warner)
- *Entertainment Weekly* (Time Warner)
- *ESPN the Magazine* (Disney)
- *Talk* (Disney)
- DC Comics (Time Warner)

[1] From http://www.pbs.org/wgbh/pages/frontline/shows/cool/giants/ "Merchants of Cool." The website cites *Brill's Content*, January 2000, pp. 99.

> "The popular arts reflect a culture they help to create."
> —William Romanowski

Film & Video
- Blockbuster Video (Viacom)
- Castle Rock Entertainment (Time Warner)
- Columbia Pictures (Sony)
- MTV Films (Viacom)
- New Line Cinema (Time Warner)
- Paramount Pictures (Viacom)
- Sony Pictures Classics (Sony)
- TriStar Pictures (Sony)
- Twentieth Century Fox (News Corp)
- Warner Brothers Studios (Time Warner)

Music
- Buena Vista Music Group (Disney)
- Columbia House (Time Warner)
- Columbia Records (Sony)
- Epic Records (Sony)
- Harmony Records (Sony)
- Hollywood Records (Disney)
- Warner Brothers Records (Time Warner)

Extra Credit: Go online and research your favorite "indie" (independent) record label. Surprise! Guess who probably owns it? If by chance it's not owned by one of the conglomerates, write the record company a letter of thanks for providing a fresh, alternative voice.

Ad Busters

Take a look at the ads from popular magazines; then read the following paragraphs and questions together as a group. Discuss your responses. Have someone record your group's ideas. Then be prepared to present your answers to the other groups.

Message/Story
Media gurus recognize that basically everything in pop culture (music, TV shows, movies, magazines, websites, print advertisements, commercials, and so forth) has a message or a point that the producer or artist is trying to get across. It sometimes comes in the form of a story: For example, a guy is walking along one day and sees a beautiful woman drinking a particular beverage; he drinks the same beverage, she is instantly attracted to him, and they live happily ever after. The message? "Drink this beverage, and women will love you."

> "I think it's unhealthy for girls to see these images of 'perfect' celebrities because photos are often airbrushed. It's not reality."
> —Faith Hill, *Glamour*, July 2003, page 199

- What is the message or story of the ad (or ads) you have in front of you?

Storyteller and Sender
Every story is presented by a storyteller—the person who brings you the message. This could be a narrator, a character, or a celebrity. But behind the storyteller is the actual sender of the message. This is the "person" (or corporation) that wants you to believe the message.

- Who is the storyteller of the ad you have in front of you?

- Who is the sender?

Methods
Senders use different methods to get their messages across. For example, they might use humor, shock, hype, or emotional melodrama to get your attention.

- What methods is the sender using in this ad?

Receiver
Senders target particular audiences (teens, retirees, girls, or skateboarders, for example) that are most likely to accept their message. Let's call them "receivers." Another word for these people is *consumers*.

- Who are the intended receivers of the message of this ad?

- How well does the sender connect with the intended receivers? In other words, does the sender use the right words or the right "look" to get the receivers' attention?

For more information on the messages behind advertising, visit
http://www.trueliesyouthtalks.com/four_lies.htm
http://www.pbs.org/wgbh/pages/frontline/shows/cool/

Response

Every message is sent for a purpose: The sender wants to influence the thoughts and behavior of the receivers. It may be as simple as getting the receiver to recognize a particular brand name or to buy a particular beverage, or as complicated as changing the receiver's attitude about sex, money—or even faith.

- How does the sender of this ad want its receivers to think or act?

Marketing Mania

As a group, come up with a marketing strategy for your assigned product and target audience. Answer the questions below; then create a poster (print advertisement or billboard) or a thirty-second skit (commercial) to market your product.

- What does your target audience value? (What do they like or dislike? What is important to them?)
- How do they dress?
- What music do they listen to?
- How do they talk? (What unique words and phrases do they use?)
- How do they spend their spare time?
- What do they have in common with your product? (This may be a stretch, but anything is possible!)
- What is the best way to get their attention? (For example: hype, humor, action, suspense, melodrama, romance, and so forth.)

Now come up with your advertisement or commercial.

The Merchants of Cool

Reflect on the video you've just watched from a Christian standpoint:

- What values are driving the "hunt for cool"? In other words, what do the "cool hunters" think is most important?

- How are those values consistent with what Jesus has to say in Matthew 6:25-34?

- As followers of Jesus, how should we respond to the messages of the media giants?

- How can Christians effectively share our message today?

- Why is the Christian message so rarely heard in pop culture today?

- When have you heard the Christian message in pop culture? How did consumers respond to it?

- Why don't we generally hear the message "Church is cool!" from the media conglomerates?

For further research on this documentary, visit
http://www.pbs.org/wgbh/pages/frontline/shows/cool/

Think About It!

- Of everything you have learned and experienced today, what has had the greatest impact on your thinking?

- What have you learned today that you didn't know before?

- How does this knowledge affect the way you think about the messages you receive from pop culture?

- How might you interact differently with pop culture as a result of what you have learned?

Read Ephesians 4:22-24.

Reflect: As Christians, we have the best of all messages to share with the world: grace and forgiveness in Jesus Christ! In fact the word *gospel* means "good news." This week, think about creative ways this message can be shared through pop culture.

SESSION 3: Product Placement

Experience

Draw lines connecting each company on the right to the movie, TV show, or video game in which it appears.*

- *Austin Powers: International Man of Mystery* (Movie)

- *Cast Away* (Movie)

- *Men in Black II* (Movie)

- *Lara Croft: Tomb Raider* (Movie)

- *American Idol* (TV Show)

- *24* (TV Show)

- *Crazy Taxi* (Video Game)

- Wilson
- Ray-Ban sunglasses
- AT&T Wireless
- Jeep Wrangler Rubicon
- Burger King
- Pizza Hut
- Sprint
- Pepsi
- Ford Motor Company
- Kentucky Fried Chicken
- FedEx
- Mercedes Benz
- Coca-Cola Company
- Starbucks
- Ford Expedition

* For more information on product placement, visit
http://entertainment.howstuffworks.com/product-placement.htm

> "You need it, we've got it—identity"
> —local department store advertisement

Product Placement: Reflections

As Christians, we have the most important "products" to pitch to the rest of the world: church, the Bible, and Jesus. We need to be aware of both the negative and positive ways that each is presented in popular culture. We can challenge others' negative attitudes about faith by asking, "Wait a minute: Are you putting down my faith because of [such-and-such movie], or because of your personal experience?"

On a personal level, we need to balance our personal faith experiences against faith as it is presented in popular media. Spend some time reflecting on the following questions:

- How much do I allow popular media and entertainment to influence my attitude toward going to church?

- reading the Bible?

- believing in Jesus?

- What attitude should I have toward church, the Bible, and Jesus?

- How can I change my attitude (if necessary)?

The Great Debate: Reflections

Does the entertainment industry reflect society, or does society reflect the entertainment industry? The answer to this question depends on how much time people spend consuming popular entertainment. The more time people spend in front of the TV, the more people reflect what they see on TV. The same goes with movies, video games, music, and other media.

"When a cartoonist named Walt Disney created a character named Bambi, deer hunting nose-dived in one year from a $5.7 million business to $1 million."

—Robert K. Johnston

- How do you spend the majority of your time?

- What are the three biggest influences (persons, activities, media, institutions such as church or school, and so on) in your life?

- What is the role of mass media and popular entertainment in your life?

- How much does your Christian faith influence your everyday life? (Think about what you wear, how you talk, what you watch and listen to, how you spend your spare time, what you buy, and so on.)

- How much time do you spend with God in prayer, Bible study, worship, service to others, or Christian fellowship?

- How might your answers to the last two questions be related?

For further information on the influences of media and entertainment, visit these websites:
http://www.changingchannels.org/effects.htm
www.trueliesyouthtalks.com/causeandeffect.htm
http://www.pbs.org/wgbh/pages/frontline/shows/cool/
http://www.aap.org/policy/re0043.html
http://www.tvturnoff.org
http://www.mediaed.org/index_html
http://www.justthink.org/resources/facts.html

Think About It!

- Of everything you have learned and experienced today, what has had the greatest impact on your thinking?

- What have you learned today that you didn't know before?

- How does this knowledge affect the way you think about the messages you receive from pop culture?

- How might you interact differently with pop culture as a result of what you have learned?

Read Philippians 4:8.

Reflect: As Christians, we are not immune to the influence of pop culture. The more time we spend exposed to pop culture without using our critical thinking skills to evaluate the messages we are receiving, the more these messages have the power to affect what we think, say, and do. Sometimes the messages we receive from the media are good and can encourage healthy behavior and faithful living. But many times those messages directly conflict with our Christian faith and experience.

SESSION 4 — Kingdom Versus Pop Culture

Scripture

You won't find the phrase *pop culture* in your Bible concordance. Nor will you find references to movies, television, hip hop, or video games. So does that mean the Bible doesn't have anything to say about pop culture? Of course not! God's Word is full of stories and instructions on how to live as faithful followers in the culture of the time, no matter where or when someone lives.

Read **Matthew 6:31-33**.

• What is Jesus saying about the culture in which we live?

Pop culture is always changing. In fact, change is the one aspect of pop culture that you can count on! Pop culture is specific to the time or era in which it's created. You might say it's temporal; it's transitory, fleeting. All cultures of the world—century after century, continent to continent—are temporal. Including ours.

> **temporal**—transitory; of this world; limited by time

Read **Psalm 103:15-18**.

There is one culture that isn't temporal, however, and that's the culture we find in the Bible. And no, we don't mean the robe-wearing, camel-riding, Hebrew-speaking kind of culture. We mean **kingdom culture**: the beliefs, customs, language, values, and even "dress," of the people of God, throughout all time and history, beyond the last age of the world. The culture found in God's kingdom is eternal. It is this kingdom culture that God calls us to be a part of first and foremost.

Read **Colossians 3:12-17**.

- Based on the passage above, what do God's people wear in God's "kingdom culture"? (verses 10, 12, and 14)

- How do they talk? (verses 8-9, and 17)

- How do they behave? (verses 13, 15, and 17)

- What kind of music do they create for God? (verse 16)

- What do they value? What attitudes and attributes are most important to them? (verses 12 and 15-16)

- Who are the celebrities in God's kingdom? (verse 17)

> **eternal:** without beginning or end; forever the same; unchanging

Until Jesus returns and we stand face to face with our loving Creator, kingdom culture must fit within the confines of the time in which we live. And if our kingdom culture faith is going to be relevant, it must express itself in and through today's popular culture.

Read **Romans 14:13-23**.

- Reword this passage so that it will speak specifically to how Christian believers should interact with today's American pop culture:

Time Machine Missionaries

Read **Matthew 28:18-20**.

This passage is known as the "Great Commission" because in it Jesus authorizes his disciples to be his representatives in the world.

> **commission:** authorization to act on behalf of another; command to perform certain duties

The word "nations" (verse 19) could also be translated "cultures." ("Go and make disciples of all cultures . . .") There are many cultures or people groups within a nation, and God calls us to share the good news with each of them—including our own American pop culture!

Mission Possible

As commissioned disciples, you are about to jump into a Time Machine and travel to the era or culture of your choice. Decide as a group where you would like to go. For example, you could visit America during the 1970's (think *The Brady Bunch*), during World War II (think *Pearl Harbor*), or the 1910's (think *Titanic*).

Once you choose a time period, brainstorm together how you will fulfill the Great Commission with the people of that time. Start by answering the following questions:

- How do the people dress? talk? behave?

- What do they do for entertainment?

- What do they value? What do they think is most important in life? What do they believe about faith, family, school, work, and citizenship?

> "So God created humankind in [God's own] image....God blessed them...."

- What is godly about this culture? Where do you see hints of God's grace and righteousness?

- What is ungodly about this culture? Where do you see selfish living and rebellion against God's ways?

- How will you follow the Great Commission and take Jesus' message to this culture? How will *you* dress and act? What words will you use? What aspects of their culture can you borrow in order to get your point across?

Bible 101

It's tempting to read one or two verses and draw a conclusion about what the Bible says about a particular topic. But focusing so much on one or two verses is like staring at only one little puzzle piece without seeing the bigger picture. (Read Leviticus 19:19, for example, for instructions on what not to wear!) Here's a formula for understanding any topic from the context of the bigger biblical story—including pop culture. The formula asks four basic questions:

- What was God's original intent?

- How did the Fall distort it?

- How did the Cross transform it?

- How are we now to live?

Read the descriptions and Scripture passages in the next sections and then answer the questions.

> "God saw everything [God] had made, and indeed, it was very good."
> —Genesis 1:27a, 28a, 31a

What Was God's Original Intent?

God created men and women in God's image (Genesis 1:26-27). One of the signs that humans are made in the image of their Creator is the desire and ability to create—meals, gardens, music, art, language, and so forth. In fact, you might say that one of our primary responsibilities as human beings is to create culture itself and to create it for the glory of God!

- What was the culture of the Garden? Think about the behavior, language, dress (!), and values of God's people (Genesis 1:28-30, 2:15-17, 2:22-25).

- What does the story of the Garden tell you about God's original intent for humankind?

How Did the Fall Distort It?

"The Fall" is a theological and practical term for when humankind (Adam and Eve) first chose to disobey God's instructions (Genesis 3). After the Fall, groups of humans separated to create individual cultures that were often at odds with one another and with God. They wanted to glorify themselves rather than God.

Read **Genesis 11:1-9**.

- What divides cultures in our time?

Despite these divisions, God chose a particular people, or culture, to bring God's message of grace to the world. Read Genesis 12:1-3. Notice in verse 3 that through Abraham and Sarah and their descendants, God intended to bless all the "families" (cultures or peoples) of the earth.

For thousands of years, the people of God lived at odds with the cultures around them. They were continually tempted to become like those cultures instead of living as a unique culture dedicated entirely to God.

Read **1 Kings 11:1-10**.

- Why does idol worship make God so angry? Why would it have been dangerous for God's people to become like the cultures that worshiped other gods?

- What are the "other gods" or "idols" of pop culture today? As persons who belong to God, how are we to interact with these idols?

How Did the Cross Transform It?

"The Cross" refers to the manner in which Jesus died—on a Roman cross as a sacrifice for the sins of the whole world. All cultures—not just the chosen people of God—are included in the plan of grace and salvation (Galatians 3:28-29). Belonging to God is no longer about following a set of cultural rules. It is a transformation of the heart in which we recognize God's loving kingship over all of our lives (Jeremiah 31:31-34). We become members of a new "culture," the kingdom of God. During his life, Jesus worked in and through the culture of his era to deliver that message.

Read **Matthew 3:1-12**.

- Whom is John talking about (verses 11-12)?

- What does he mean by saying, "The kingdom of heaven has come near" (verse 2)?

How Are We Now to Live?

Jesus' life, death, and resurrection paved the way for the transforming power of the Holy Spirit in the life of every believer. We are no longer slaves to what the world values but servants in the kingdom of God.

- The early Christians, empowered by the Holy Spirit, lived lives that were so totally different from the world around them that they even drew the attention of powerful political figures. Paul, one of the earliest Christian missionaries, spoke before rulers and kings about God's grace for all people. (For example, Acts 26:19-20.)

- Read Titus 2:11-14. What does it mean for you to live "in the present age" a life that is "self-controlled, upright, and godly" (verse 12)? Be specific.

Think About It!

- Of everything you have learned today what has had the greatest impact on your thinking?

- Which Scripture verse that you read today was the most memorable? Why?

- How can you fulfill the Great Commission (Matthew 28:18-20) within the popular culture of your generation?

The "kingdom culture" of Christ should be evident in every aspect of our lives: the clothes we wear, the music we listen to, the movies and TV shows we watch, the art and music we create, the games we play, and so on. To claim our identity as "kingdom people" doesn't mean that we "Christianize" all of those things, but that we ask ourselves:

- **By watching this movie or wearing this outfit (or you name it), am I bringing myself closer to God or pushing myself further away?**

- **By participating in this activity or behaving in this manner, am I bringing others closer to God, or pushing them away?**

- **How can I express God's grace to others through this experience?**

SESSION 5: Christianity and Pop Culture

Tradition — Thinking Theologically

Christians throughout the centuries have been at odds with popular culture. Beginning with the persecution of Christians in the first, second, and third centuries, Christians have had to take a stand against those aspects of popular culture that didn't line up with the basic tenets of the Christian faith.

As the centuries wore on, Christians were sometimes at the heart of popular culture, as with the Catholic Church in Medieval times, or on the fringes, as with the monks of that same era. Thus, different denominations and faith traditions have developed different approaches or attitudes toward popular culture over time, many of which are still prevalent today.

It can be helpful to lump these approaches into five categories. These categories fall on a continuum that looks something like this:

Most open to culture | assimilate — consume — engage — appropriate — condemn | Least open to culture

- **assimilate:** to absorb; to be indistinguishable from

    Q: When have you been unable to identify persons who were Christian by the music they listened to, TV shows they watched, clothes they wore, and so on?

- **consume:** to pick and choose from a number of options; choosing some but not others

    Q: When have you seen examples of Christians who were selective in what they would and would not consume from pop culture? (For example, they'll listen to some non-Christian CDs but not all.)

- **engage:** to involve someone; to have a two-way conversation

    Q: When have you seen examples of Christians who, like Paul in Athens, selected certain messages from pop culture then responded with their own message of faith in Christ?

- **appropriate:** to take for one's own use

    Q: When have you seen examples of Christians who borrowed musical styles or clothing from pop culture to communicate a Christian message?

- **condemn:** to disapprove; to censure

    Q: When have you seen examples of Christians who condemned something in pop culture (movies, music)—even to the point of boycotting companies, artists, or products?

Match Up

Draw a line pairing the scenario on the left with the Christian approach to popular culture on the right that best defines it.

- In the 1930s, the Episcopalian Committee on Motion Pictures and the Catholic Legion of Decency insisted that their members "remain away from all motion pictures except those which do not offend decency and Christian morality."

- The Apostle Paul affirmed to the people of Athens that they were "extremely religious." He then went on to use the words of a popular Greek poet to explain how Jesus was the "unknown god" they were seeking (Acts 17:22-32).

- The Desert Fathers and other cloistered communities of the first, second, and third centuries refused to participate in the popular entertainments of the day.

- The Catholic Church in Medieval times *was* popular culture; Christianity was the state religion of many nations, setting the standards for behavior, dress, speech, music, art—even food.

- Martin Luther and the Reformers of the 1500s set their hymns to the tunes of popular drinking songs.

- **Condemn**

- **Appropriate**

- **Assimilate**

- **Engage**

- **Consume**

Christ and Culture[1]

In 1951 a theologian named H. Richard Niebuhr published a landmark book entitled *Christ and Culture*. It looks at five different ways Christians view their relationship with the world. Is the world all evil? Is it all good? Is it some mixture of both? And how are Christians supposed to interact with the culture of the world around them?

Niebuhr puts the church's various approaches to culture in five categories, which run on a continuum from far '"left" to far "right." The two "left-of-center" views tend to downplay evil and overemphasize good in the world, while the two "right-of-center" views tend to downplay the good and overemphasize evil in the world. In each category are listed Christian traditions that lean toward that worldview, as well as key literary, historical, philosophical or theological persons from the Christian faith who have held that view. (If you haven't heard of any of them, that's OK. Your teacher probably hasn't either. But trust us: they're important!)

Place the views on this continuum as you read their descriptions:

Where would you place the two quotations above on this continuum?

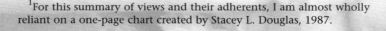

[1] For this summary of views and their adherents, I am almost wholly reliant on a one-page chart created by Stacey L. Douglas, 1987.

"Left-of-Center" Views

- **Christ of Culture:** This viewpoint says that the world is good. Christ is in all aspects of culture. You can be part of culture and enjoy all that it has to offer. Traditions within this category include Gnostics, old liberals, and Marxist Christians. Key figures include Thomas Jefferson, Immanuel Kant, and Alfred, Lord Tennyson.

    Q: Where does this view fall on the continuum we've already discussed? Which approach does it use? (assimilate, consume, engage, appropriate, or condemn?)

- **Christ above Culture:** This viewpoint says the world is either neutral, or "less than good." The Christian is to be separate and slightly "above" the world. But the Christian sees Christ in all that is good in culture. This category includes Roman Catholics, Anglicans, and liberal Baptists. Key figures include St. Thomas Aquinas, Mother Teresa, and C.S. Lewis.

    Q: Where does this view fall on the continuum we've already discussed? Which approach does it use?

"Center" View

- **Christ transforms Culture:** This viewpoint says that the world is both good and evil. Culture is tainted with sin, but is changeable. The world can be made a better place if sin is dealt with in a meaningful way. This category includes Calvinists (Reformed, Presbyterian) and Wesleyans (Methodists, holiness traditions). Key figures include St. Augustine of Hippo, John Calvin, and John Wesley.

    Q: Where does this view fall on the continuum we've already discussed? Which approach does it use?

"Right of Center" Views

- **Christ in tension with Culture:** This viewpoint says that the world is basically evil. The Christian has to balance being obedient to God and living in a sinful world. Traditions within this category include Lutherans, some Charismatic traditions, and Neo-Orthodoxy. Key figures include Martin Luther, Dietrich Bonhoeffer, and Karl Barth.

   Q: Where does this view fall on the continuum we've already discussed? Which approach does it use?

- **Christ against Culture:** This view says that, because of the evil in the world, Christians should not participate in culture; they are to be wholly separate. Traditions within this category include the monastic, Mennonite, and Friends (Quaker) traditions, as well as fundamentalist Charismatic traditions. Key figures include Tertullian, St. Benedict, Bob Jones, Jerry Falwell, and Jimmy Swaggart.

   Q: Where does this view fall on the continuum we've already discussed? Which approach does it use?

Ask Your Pastor

Your leader may decide to invite a member of your pastoral staff to visit your class and answer the questions below. (If not, contact a member of your pastoral staff and ask to set up a time to interview him or her. You might want to give a copy of the student book to your pastor beforehand, so that he or she will know what you have been studying.)

- Where does our denomination fall on the continuum?

- How does our church's view affect its stance on issues related to pop culture (such as violence and sex in the media, for example)?

- What is the official stance of our denomination on issues relating to popular culture?

- How about its stance on such things as parental advisory ratings for movies and video games?

- Does our denomination have any resources for teaching media literacy? If so, what are they? If not, why?

- Has our denomination issued any statements or requests to the media conglomerates? Why or why not? If so, what were those statements?

Resources expressing various denominational or historical views toward media and popular culture:
http://www.changingchannels.org/denom.htm#1
http://www.pcusa.org/ega/aboutus.htm
http://gbgm-umc.org/UMhistory/Wesley/advice.html
The United Methodist Church 2000 Book of Resolutions, ¶113

Think About It!

- Of everything you have learned and experienced today, what has had the greatest impact on your thinking?

- What have you learned today that you didn't know before?

- Where do you see yourself on the continuum of responses to pop culture?

- How should the church fulfill its calling to be "salt" and "light" in pop culture? (Matthew 5:13-16)

- What role can you play in fulfilling that calling?

Quiz Time

SESSION 6 — Thinking Theologically

As a personal challenge, answer the following questions as best you can:

1. What are the four components of the Wesleyan Quadrilateral?

2. Why is it important that we use all four components of the Quadrilateral in discerning God's truth, not just one or two?

3. Name something you learned in Session Two (Reason) that you didn't know before. How does this knowledge affect the way you think about the messages of pop culture?

4. What was the main activity you did for Session Three (Experience)? Based on your experience with that activity, how much do you think pop culture influences what you think, say, and do?

5. What are the primary differences between "kingdom culture" and pop culture?

6. List two Bible passages that were a part of this study that you don't remember having heard before.

7. Of the five Christian approaches to pop culture (assimilate, consume, engage, appropriate, condemn), which one resonates the most with you? Why?

8. Name one thing you learned from this study that you'll never forget.

9. As a result of this study, how will you change the way you interact with pop culture?

Going to God in Worship

Welcome, Introductions, and Announcements

Call to Worship (from Psalm 90:1-2)

> **Leader:** Lord, you have been our dwelling place in all generations.
> **Class:** Before the mountains were brought forth,
>   or ever you had formed the earth and the world,
> **All:** From everlasting to everlasting you are God.

Invocation by Worship Leader

> Dear Lord, you have called us together to reflect on all that we have learned about pop culture and to consecrate ourselves to you. Speak to our hearts through your Word and through your community gathered here. Amen.

Songs of Praise

Scripture Reading

- Luke 12:22-32
- Galatians 5:16-25

Prayers of Confession

Write on a 3x5 index card one way that you have allowed yourself to be negatively influenced by pop culture and have acted in opposition to God's "kingdom culture." Fold the card and place it in the basket as it is passed. When the basket is brought forward, pray together:

> Most merciful God, we confess that we have allowed pop culture to tell us what and in whom to believe and how we are to live. We have turned to media instead of your Word for guidance. Forgive us—we are truly sorry. Help us to see beyond our own culture to your kingdom culture. Grant that we may take our delight in you and live to the glory of your name. Amen.

Expression of Forgiveness

Leader *(holding up the basket of index cards)*: Dear ones, the Bible promises that "If we confess our sins, he who is faithful and just and will forgive us our sins and cleanse us from all unrighteousness" (1 John 1:9). That is good news! We have a fresh start. We are no longer bound to the sinful messages and attitudes of pop culture, but are free to live as "kingdom people" according to God's good plan for our lives in Christ.
All: Thanks be to God! Amen.

Scripture Reading

- Matthew 10:16
- Ephesians 5:15-20

Songs of Encouragement

Student Testimonies

Holy Communion

Time of Dedication

During this time, you will be invited to participate in laying-on of hands for each student as a way of supporting one another.

The pastor or leader will pray:

God of all, we consecrate this your servant, *(name)*. Empower *(her or him)* by your Holy Spirit to be "wise as a serpent and innocent as a dove" (Matthew 10:16) as *(she or he)* interacts with pop culture. Help *(her or him)* to embrace those who are honestly seeking you in pop culture. Give *(her or him)* creativity to discern how *(she or he)* can affect pop culture in ways that affirm the values of your kingdom. In the name of the Creator, the Son, and the Holy Spirit. Amen.

Benediction (from 1 Thessalonians 5:23)

All: May the God of peace sanctify you entirely; and may your spirit and soul and body be kept sound and blameless at the coming of our Lord Jesus Christ. Amen.

Journaling Option

Find a place in the building or outside on the church grounds where you can be alone. If possible, find a place at least 20 feet from the nearest person. Commit to silence for this time of reflection.

Opening Prayer

God, guide us as we worship you, that we might reflect your glory and the splendor of your creation. Help us to listen for your voice in stillness and silence, that we may better understand your will for our lives. Guard us from the darkness of sin and despair as we commit our hearts and minds to you through Jesus Christ, your Son and our Savior. Amen.

Scripture Readings:

- Matthew 10:16
- Philippians 4:4-9

Readings for Reflection

Even in the church, theological discussion is often more likely to happen following a movie than a sermon.[1]
—Robert K. Johnston in *Reel Spirituality: Theology and Film in Dialogue*

In one survey, three-fourths of single Christian adults thought "movies containing vulgarities, explicit sex, nudity, and antibiblical messages had an adverse effect on their moral and spiritual condition," but at least half of these same people approved of films that included these very ingredients.... Despite fears and warnings about the potential dangers of the entertainment media, most people believe they are personally immune.[2]
—William Romanowski in *Eyes Wide Open: Looking for God in Popular Culture*

The great sin of most of the stories of popular culture—in film, television, novels, and the like—is not that they are violent or obscene or godless, but that they waste our time. Since I can hear only so many stories in my life, why settle for anything less than the best ones?[3]
—Daniel Taylor, as quoted in *The Christian Imagination: The Practice of Faith in Literature and Writing*

My dear friends, let every man, every woman among you, deal honestly with yourselves. Ask your own heart, "What am I seeking day by day? What am I desiring? What am I pursuing? Earth or heaven? The things that are seen, or the things that are not seen?" What is your object, God or the world? As the Lord liveth, if the world is your object, still all your religion is vain.
—John Wesley in his Sermon #113, "The Difference Between Walking by Sight and Walking by Faith"

Written Reflection

- What jumped out at you as you read the above Scriptures and readings? Why?

- What thoughts do these readings spark in your mind that you have never considered before?

---

[1]From *Reel Spirituality: Theology and Film in Dialogue* by Robert K. Johnston; (Baker Academic, a division of Baker Book House Company, 2000); page 24.
[2]From *Eyes Wide Open: Looking for God in Popular Culture* by William Romanowski; (Brazos Press, a division of Baker Book House Company, 2001); pages 30-31.
[3]From *The Christian Imagination: The Practice of Faith in Literature and Writing* by Leland Ryken; (WaterBrook Press, 2002); page 417.

Think About It!

- If you had to state the key learnings of this entire study in one sentence, what would you say?

- What do you think Jesus means when he commands us to be "wise as serpents and innocent as doves" (Matthew 10:16)? How does this relate to how you interact with pop culture?

- Where have you heard God's voice in movies, TV shows, music, and so forth?

- How have you failed to listen to God's voice amid the many clamoring voices of pop culture?

- Make a list on a separate sheet of paper of what you can do every day, every week, and every year to better hear God's voice.

- What can you do to make sure God's voice is heard in and through pop culture?